Peter Bradbury

By the same author

MONTEREY CYPRESS
Lachlan Mackinnon

Chatto & Windus   LONDON

Published in 1988 by
Chatto & Windus Ltd
30 Bedford Square
London WC1B 3RP

A CIP catalogue record for this book is available from the British Library.

ISBN 0 7011 3264 7

Some of these poems have previously appeared, sometimes in different
form, in *Acumen Magazine, The Honest Ulsterman, London Magazine,
London Review of Books, The New Review, The New Statesman, The
P.N. Review*, and *The Times Literary Supplement*.
    Seven of these poems appeared in *New Chatto Poets* (1986).
    A collection containing many of these poems received an Eric Gregory
Award in 1986, and four appeared in *The Gregory Poets 1985–6*
(Salamander Press/Penguin Books).

Photoset by
Rowland Phototypesetting Ltd
Bury St Edmunds, Suffolk

Printed in Great Britain by
Redwood Burn Ltd
Trowbridge, Wiltshire

For Sarah, Jessica and Lachlan

Contents

I

Loose Connections

I was either going mad or becoming
a schoolmaster when I woke with the question
Distinguish between Fred Karno's Army
and Alexander's Ragtime Band put fiercely to me
by a voice that sounded like conscience dreaming

of an exemplary, excessive scruple. Perhaps
my addiction to crosswords, wordplay,
arcana . . . This afternoon, an ellipsis
between one morning and another,
I feel the nineteenth-century amplitude

and lassitude of *Brewer's Phrase and Fable*,
not that that helped, and as I drift off to sleep
I see your kicked-off plimsolls' tongues are lolling
like dogs', beached on a dry stretch of the lawn
beyond the splash-range of the paddling-pool,

the lawn itself sprouting a white five o'clock
shadow of daisies . . . Yet it is young, younger
and greener daily, and the daisies are white
horses foaming towards an unfamiliar
welcoming shore where you stand like Nausikaa

who dressed the stranger, asking him no questions
but telling him, rather, that to escape them
he should go on towards the palace, wait
in the cool of her father's orchard until he reckoned
she'd be home and then come on in for supper.

Handcarts

I put my foot down and discovered a city,
an ant pushing an egg like a refugee's handcart,
another, a serious pram-race, touching
antennae to taste one another's terror.

The little shops have been broken open and spill
souvenirs and newspapers on the pavement.
Such redemptive, peripheral sadness while the black
militia point our feet toward the outskirts.

'We walked between columns of smoke. Nobody dreamed
of the immaculate, brick-by-brick restoration
of the Old Quarter, the university,
the medieval ghetto, the Catholic shrine.'

They were back within minutes, working like Trojans
or Germans, jobbing builders, entrepreneurs
and their parasites, ragpickers and dudes with knives . . .
by-blows of the queen ant's lethal forgetfulness.

Blooms

I

There is a dead frog on the lawn, glistening,
untouchable. At first we think of the cat,
our guardsmanlike water-bailiff, and indeed
he will have fished it out, but this creature
has been flattened by some disaster.
Deduction travels slowly backwards
like Theseus to our infant daughter
plonking brick-ends into the splashy pond.
The frog must have risen as we hope our souls might
through the mucky layers to open light.

II

The shrub stoops to us, but is still taller
than the kitchen door plus the steps. The more it sheds
of its pink bell-shaped flowers, sized and flared
like the candleholders on a child's birthday cake,
the more it blooms, seemingly inexhaustible.
This would be a child some centuries old.
No perfectionist, it excels itself
daily, each morning brighter than the last.

A Winter's Tale

A dying winter light
sharpens our hearing,
late warblers on the other bank
jabber and jab
at the low skimming midges

Keats noted here.
The wind travelled upstream
and vanished, hours back.
All the bluster gone out of it,
the bruised land

gathers its browns and purples
in clumsy
wickerwork tangles.
Across the slimy path
to the kingfisher's nesting-place

the dogwood planted last year
has taken hold,
dug in, as though
the tangles were barbed wire,
this river not

an English river, we
not coming up the tame bank
with the stop
and start of our toddler
picking up stones.

That was the war
that choked the water-meadow,
took off the hands
and scattered mud
in ephemeral channels

there, where those haggard saplings
are sucking the soil dry.
We read our history
in the melting horizon; that,
and our uncertain future.

Pasternak Weather

The clouds relax and bulge.
The wind gives a last puff, the last
dab of the powder-puff
before an actor makes his entrance

and then it comes,
sudden, saddening, sodden,
crossing out distance
like a censor's pencil

and driving us
in to watch beads
like ruffled sparrows
take cover beneath window-frames.

Their shivering
exhausts them and they drop,
even the last, who see the sun
break through like invisible ink.

October

We have lived in small towns hard by the sea.
Even the lorries
seemed to have come to take the waters,
stiff-spined
in the difficult streets.

The woods thrashed like tethered water,
the municipal paddling-pool
spilled in the browned, nervous hands
of our estuary coast.
Stale ocean backed up into fresh,

the dry, miniature gullies filled and pulsed
like a frog's web under a microscope.
The world was glistening with wet.
When the old men speak of your promise,
remember that it is not made to them.

In Beauchamp Place

A girl in a fawn mac ducks into a taxi.
The day creaks and whines like a steel halyard.
It bangs the mast. It wants to set sail

but the shiny cars jostle like floes
in the choked tumultuous neck of a river.
Their voices rise. They are geese in a head-wind.

You remember raking the river-bed, the light
that broke round your boots, the tin cans
you struck for in the clouds of dislodged mud

every stuck hank of weed let go.
The wind off the hills forked like water
round the splash and splash of your clawed rake

and you stood in the silence of your work
watching the dripped light swooshed away
like the lights changing in a rainy crowded street.

Fallodon Wood

As I walked out one weekday by the knots of tussock-sedge
which has gripped down a hundred years into the mud
of the wetlands men were labouring to conserve
I saw them busy round a tree whose wrinkled trunk

threw up whippy suckers among the reeds
like the parable about wheat and tares. The sower.
It was a recent import, some Siberian
willow, a sappy brittle wood that gave sharply

with a crackle anticipating flames, a recoil spray
of shavings and a silence before bow-saws
twanged as they stripped the fallen limbs.
There's a rub in the grain and splinter of that wood –

it's not mine, or yours, or any of ours –
that says what it is to grow up in foreignness,
warp to that weather and become at home –
if wood can say what wood is, as we wish to and cannot.

From a French Court

Gentlemen of the jury, you have heard
all these ignorant experts call me a lost
soul or poor martyred child; don't take their word
and gaol my mother and her man. At least
imagine. When the shrinks heard how I'd lived
I was an ocean into which they dived
like people snorkelling on holiday.
Small wonder if they found the monstrous forms
their blueprints had prepared them for in swarms
and called them mine, my thoughts in disarray.

I know what you are thinking. You are thinking,
'The poor lamb, he still wants the monsters freed.'
You purr with tender understanding, thinking
and understanding nothing. Oh, I read
your hardened hearts. You wouldn't keep a dog
chained to a bed or tethered to the bog,
but you've not broken like my mother did
when she was jacked in by a married lover
who ran for wifey like a mouse for cover
at the first sniff of this unwanted kid.

He stormed out to preserve his family
from contact with a cow, said when she'd calved
he'd kill her if she blabbed. It wasn't me
but him in me she beat and burned and starved.
Why did she plunge my hands in boiling water?
Because I wouldn't eat? A battered daughter
who acts like that should get what she deserves,
seven years hard and no remission, that
is what you think. You haven't seen the flat
in which my mother lived on her nerves

while I went to a minder's for the years
in which they've told you the crucial bonds are made
or, as in my case, not. I have. The smears
of mould still well up in my dreams. I played
listlessly, and my mother hardly spoke
until one day she rolled up with this bloke
and said I'd not be coming any more.
They would be moving for his work, you see.
The minder missed the cash, but hardly me.
They took me to a house I never saw.

We arrived late and I was half-asleep,
four years old, too tired for an appetite.
She gave me bread, and I began to weep
and threw it on the floor. It was that night
she boiled my hands until the skin peeled off.
She did it with a kind of crying laugh.
He was unpacking, I suppose. Not there.
When he came in and saw my fingers stuck
together he was white and hit her. *Fuck,
oh fuck*, she gasped, *just hide him, anywhere.*

We'll sort things out tomorrow. That tomorrow
has not yet come. I don't know what was said,
if anything, in anger or in sorrow,
but lived through eight years tethered to a bed
by day, a lavatory by night. I spent
a week alone at ten, the week they went
on holiday, a trip they'd planned through months
of putting by and making do. A bare
twist of bread and a crust of Camembert
were left me, hardly what you'd call a lunch.

I slept, though. You can't cry every night
or even want to. You get used to waiting.
When I escaped, I couldn't read or write

or use a fork. Two years in care, relating
to others, as they call it, have taught me much
but now, I beg you, put us back in touch.
I've grown new skin. It fits me like a glove
and I can feel things better. Man and wife,
they are my life, my only shot at life;
only they can teach me how to love.

Canticle

You wipe the tears from your mirror's
amnesia, freshly bathed and shaved.

Imagine a hand, a pencil imagining
the flesh of first love, how the skin
drinks and disperses light. You made appointments
but you knew only you would be there
and you pushed down the thought of such a meeting.

*

A gallery of abstracts
in a city of galleries and bridges. Suddenly sick,
you spun out on the windy walkway where your vertigo
vanished. There was no feeling you might leap to be fought
    down.

We are not gods but witnesses
and you were more moved by the hard, the brassy come-on
of a milkmaid who has stared out two centuries
or the curls on a girl's nape
immortally imperilled by her ravisher.

*

Her skin drank and dispersed the light
– Mediterranean, unreachable with her back to the bench
and her legs stretched out along the earth. A shadow
dims her face in the photograph, blackens her black hair.
She is singed by the flames of longing, *veteris
vestigia flammae*, as you thought she was, she would be.
Yours the impotent chatter of a moth against the glass.

*

In a city of bridges, girders and marshalling-yards
like all the explanations you have ever heard
for everything. You have explained yourself as many ways

as the lines branching south or the lines branching
from your hand's heel into your palm. The grim
    technician's
frown as he wrestles with the junction-box of lights,
those analytic cannibal dismemberments you spun from
and out of fear,
a rumour of trains in the penetrated earth.

                              *

At your window
a dead white moth folds its hands, the orison of an effigy.

What lives is warm, is legs
stretched out along the earth, warming and being warmed,
what lives, lives
as long as you
write, and your fate is in your hand.

                              *

A man in exile
— you imagined his single bag's razor, toothbrush
and dictionary —
said that love is minute attention
and wants to change the world, so you imagined
his first evening in any city

making his way to harbours, to canals,
anything that might ever change to rain,
earth's native tongue that gives our skins their proper
    names,

as the awkward homemaking of the hermit crab.

                              *

The girl you kicked leaves with in her red jacket days
is dead. You don't know if you loved her

but you hope all the dead whom you have loved
are blind
and you fear they see more,
more clearly.
Look at the sense their lives make!

*

The exile is impervious
to the dialects of your language.

It is high time you were moving
on, to the country place
you don't possess.

The orchard there is overgrown, overthrown
by a low shrub with vivid scarlet leaves.

*

In the flat space of painting
in the flat space of writing
the stories of the dead
can be told with no explanation, explanation
being only a bridge towards the future
they do not have.

Living eyes close like galleries
to harbour dreams of apple-blossom,
hillsides of tossing snow.

*

All love is first love,
there, unreachable, there. Your mirrored face.

Wipe the tears from your mirror's
amnesia, see
your figure in its landscape
where the soul's precipice is a walkable windy walkway.

Move awkwardly
into the foreign, the unexplained future you did not expect.
Galleries and marshalling-yards,
their unsettled cohabitation
your country place.

Feel the earth which is not the earth beneath
within you, rising,
and stretch your legs along that earth,
be warmed, tan in the sun of longing.
Feel the sky curving to its new horizon.

You will be at home in your way with words.

All love is first love,
there, unreachable, there.

Of Making Many Books There Is No End

A day of tourism and sleepy pears.
The pub by the river has closed its terrace
so we sit in the lounge. The angel fish
are out of puff to blow us the kisses
they so try to, exhausted gaiety girls . . .

II

Cambridge

I was tiny once, under these wide skies,
but last night's ghost was a girl with a clarinet,
her foot tapping the floor.

Yesterday, the train kicked up leaves
like snow today's rain will melt down again.

Fences that couldn't pretend to keep the wind out
kept one horse in, a horse with spindly legs.

It is a cold North European city
where I wake to the thrum of tyres on asphalt,
a demand as infinite as the sky's.

I would wander like her breath through that clarinet.

Flamingo

Polished, the copper ashtray
holds strange reflected shapes,
swarthy, Egyptian. It is not
self-righteous, not gold
these humble, hammered surfaces.
When I hold up my lighter to it
it sees, through the mist,
a lost flamingo
stalking the freshets
for elver and minnow.
It is my childhood's estuary.
What is happening?
I do not know. The gravelled water
flutes at his ankles, and is cold.

A Family Tradition

My name has no meaning certified;
is it *warlike man*
or *one from across the water*?
I cannot ask my ancestors,
who heard it newly minted and barely
applicable to men, it was so strange;

to me, it is what I have carried
since I first answered to it.
It has seemed a flint
picked up on some shore,
with its smoky heart and rubbed edges
skipping the water until it smacks

into the breaker of a southern tongue,
the tongue I voice in.
When I pronounce it, I am leaning
toward the sealed future, which hears
better than we, to my unconceived son calling
"Lachlan, Lachlan".

Cairn

There is time for the child to be mistaken.

In his encyclopaedia, a snub-nosed ICBM
rises like a milk-bottle from its silo
in the artist's uncomplicated vision.

His olive plastic soldiers shift their terrain
from the waxed red tiles of the kitchen floor
to a cairn of rubble inside the gateless gateway
to the coppice he calls a jungle,

to the miniature caves of Borneo or Malaya.
It is too late for Suez and too soon for Aden.

He stands in the wilderness and cries *I want
to go home, I want to go home*
when he is home, a happy, protected child.

A landslip seals his soldiers' fate and tomb.
Going back, he would stand by his own

he comes to feel, feeling the knobbly belts
on plastic soldiers while he queues
to buy a helicopter for his daughter.

Baby Bunting

The tall policeman
smiles from his taller horse.
'So your mother's alone?
I'll be around.' The coarse

not-in-front-of-the-children chuckle
of his chum on the pavement
only adds to the pickle
I never meant.

I never speak to strangers.
How should I know
my voice is louder than I think?

My friend won't go.
He is ogling the horse's harness,
the truncheon on its flank.

Southampton

Two squirrels
hightail it up a tree.

Grey fools,
it's only me,

but almost twenty years have charred
to stubble on my chin

since I saw you in our backyard
in Michigan

the evening we arrived.
Immigrants, how you've thrived,

like the kid who couldn't play baseball
or count a general's stars

but in a year's absence
forgot the names of British cars.

Stirring Times in 1963

I was put into Grade 2D. For half an hour
after lunch we'd to put our heads down on our arms
and rest at our desks. We were supervised
by a senior, usually a girl, who kept us silent.
Seven years old, we couldn't see the point of this
so we liked Tessa best, who'd let us talk.
She was taken off duty. That day, when we crocodiled
from the lower to the upper school where the dining-hall
    was
for lunch, we had heard the news. We demonstrated
with shouts of 'We want Tessa! We want Tessa!'
People hung out of windows goggling
at the unheard-of din that went unpunished.
That was the spirit of the times.
Five years later the black riots came within blocks
of the comfy clapboard house we had rented that year,
my parents' friends wrote with some disbelief.
I'd been brought back to England to be struck
by a car and learn twenty years on
that what had dimmed half my twenties
was that and other accidents
– not, as I'd hoped, my generation's restlessness.

Seventy-Second Air Force

'Kits'
are *models*,
the word for transfers is 'decals'
and six feet scale down to an inch.

All the pilots were six feet tall.
I dotted their faces flesh,
which is fifteen parts white
to one each of red and yellow.

They must be modern,
they must be military,
they were largely American.
My best were nothing like the real thing
I implored to be taken to
on open days.

Heyford and Alconbury,
Lakenheath, Mildenhall
and Bentwaters
with its air of refraction,

these were the names. And these,
Phantom, Intruder, Voodoo
– stub wings like a bird's broken wings! –
withdrawn asthmatic passions
that could not
                    tear these beauties from their purpose.

Carnal Knowledge

I would use up three pens a term.
I bent my nibs
into an eagle's tearing
and rending bill.
They would splutter and stop.
If I believe in omens
it will have been a warning, it will make
sense of what happened next.

Cigarettes in the trespassed garden
with another boy's girl-friend. She went home
down the hill through the tall woods.
Astray, lingering, fearful,
I watched the prickling of the stars
where the bushy November clouds drew back.
The trees kept brushing over them
like knowing I too had a home to go to.

Here

The disappearance of time, a life as orderly
as the formal view with its row of poplars
and the sleeping river, which at the mill
was brilliance but now has found its level
lower, less limber; these and these alone

are offered by this city with no echoes
where leaves by the cathedral murmur
obliquely their little snide exclusions
and the tobacconists remember the dead.
A woman here would be housed among women,

making love and a tray of muffins
with the same tranquillised complacency –
or say wildly, *When I was sent for mending
I was limp and unbuttoned, torn by carelessness:
now, light shines through the pinpricks in my arms.*

This is a man's world of leather bindings
and football posts bowled down by swinging children.
A file of boys appears in the early mist,
shuffling to showers, muddied, jogging half-crouched
as though they feared the mist would turn to gas.

Monterey Cypress

The tall sad house
blew open every spring
– gusts from the street,
a dusty hall

where the telephone was
that never rang
with invitations
I waited in for.

The tall sad tree
behind the house
was dying, brown
in patches

where the fungus had bitten,
shabby
as a camouflaged helmet
on a parade-ground

and lonely,
stranger than us,
a foreigner
from California.

A lightning-conductor
we both felt,
and surely one
for sorrow.

The Suitcase

Last thing, after the doors, the windows
and the light in the hall, I come up
and for fear the cat might stifle the baby
I put the suitcase across the stairs.

We are walled in by dreams of travel.
I know that by now every city
has its village of exiles, conspiring
over chess in the back rooms of bookshops.

The voices of the street rise to our window,
few of them human. We fall asleep.
Life is not a permit to live
but a ball of fur sticking in my throat.

It is brown and covered with labels
and we keep the blankets for guests in it.
I touch it every night, I do it
last thing, after the doors, the windows.

Circles

'I am tormented by abstractions.
Sometimes I can't remember where I am
and I have to haul my eyes round the walls
and furniture to find out who I'm with
and whatever it was I was
talking about . . .

'I am tormented by abstractions.
The world must be imagined to exist
and my imagination's failing.
It all goes faint, the walls, the furniture . . .
even my wife does, and whatever
she cares about.'

Crystals

You remember chemical transformations
vaguely, in the prehistory before exams
counted for much. They were done in the wooden lab that
    smelt
of dangerous acids, comical ether
– somebody passed out, having soaked his handkerchief.
The best was copper sulphate, gathering
its crystal round the necessary thread.
Are crystals held together by flaws?
Chemical transformations! and the result of one is
you wake up in tears and can do nothing all day.

Low Water

The sea toys with its food, pushes it
to the side of its plate; planks, oilcans,
dead handkerchiefs. The sea has grown up
into some terrible kind of slob.
It watches too much television.
It slurps the froth off its drink without looking.
Its analyst recommends a change
but it has no plans to go anywhere,
do anything. It lolls. Gulls pick at the leavings
in its lap as it drowses past lighting-up time.

Its vast lethargy crumbles stones and shells.
We hardly dare speak of survival
though survival is what it has achieved.
We hold hands, the first time in weeks;
what I should wear to my doctor
was the last dilemma I teased you with,
a torchbeam in the fog around my thoughts.
This great torpor is the prelude to cure.
We may yet hear the sound we came for,
the sea stirring, rattling its bars of shingle.

III

In the Luxembourg Gardens

I

Children sailed toy yachts in the pool
with their fathers helping, itching
to take the helm. On two chairs pulled together
a man lay in his vest asleep. Flowers

shouted back at the sun, much louder
than any human din, just as the concierge
at my hotel this morning
was less responsive than the hot water tap.

Maybe what's irked her is the woman in the next room
on honeymoon, her voice with money in it, money
lingering for a death or two, her deep laugh
undercutting the husband's thinner buzz.

Yesterday afternoon, their second, they came in
having a mild spat, quickly settled. Followed
growing mastery in his tone, a silence,
and then her generous, her grateful cries,

an exiled, virtuoso cellist
suddenly rising through the café orchestra.
There is nothing so homesick-making
as the ecstasy of a fellow transient.

II

I fall back on my bed and smoke,
watching the smoke uncurling through the window
like someone ambling with a purpose,
a date or interview he's early for.

I've laid the bourbon in for your arrival,
there's nothing else; another morning
à la Bibliothèque Nationale,
another lunch at what's become my café,

and I'll make the airport with time in hand.
After dinner, I understood
the heaviness
in my heart was the longing

the sense of not belonging here
incites, inflames. If flowers
have a folk-memory, those flowers will know
empires and republics rise and fall

like water in a fountain, but the sound
of children hasn't changed. Neither perhaps
is the history of human feelings possible,
though every feeling has a history.

August 23rd

Heroes are everywhere. This plaque says
the workers of Paris en pleine
insurrection and so forth seized La Bourse
du Travail four days before Liberation.

There is some kind of muddle
when we come out under the Arc de Triomphe;
like a flower-bed or a gas-repair
the Unknown Soldier has been roped off

for the arrival of the honour-guard, which slowly
clots at the heart of a knot of uniforms
to be led out, the back pair's epaulettes and sabres
shuffling to line up with the heavy boots and combat
     jackets

of the two in front with machine-guns. They all
stare blankly at the city, wind riffles the flowers on the slab
as it shakes itself out of the giant flag above us,
the officer kisses his sword and goes.

I mention behind every seventh tree or so
outside the U.S. Embassy stood men and one woman
with flak-jackets and loaded magazines. Riot police.
Evening darkened their dark wire-windowed vans in side-
     streets

but not so black as the muzzle that looked straight through
     me.
Neither fantasy nor reality but the in-between of waking.
There's one street, I think it's in the Marais, thin,
a little twisted, mainly kosher restaurants, where some

seventy-five thousand Jews were gathered for collection
– almost double the size of our home town –
and a new plaque commemorates the victims
of an attack within newspaper-reading memory;

it was there I saw the two Vietnamese
Jews in yarmulkes like an unhealed wound.
What is the past? The plaque to Mistinguett
above the policewoman in the El Al office door,

one where Jaurès was blown away, one
to an American who died in the Resistance,
the sober lines of the statue of Auguste Comte
or a loaded gun? Liberated, it is endless.

La Place de la République

Coaches drop the English
au pairs from Belgium here
like caviar, my love,
the year you did it.

The Republic stares west, lit only
by the flares of a fun-fair:
dodgems, a shooting-gallery,
burgers and fries.

The last years of the century
stare at us with the bright
wild eyes of the younger sister's
black face twirled in the carousel.

Only the fountain is true
silver, blown by the wind
of early autumn
into a bridal veil.

Here all our journeys start
and end. You gone, I read. White wine.
Our one day out of Paris
together was Versailles. To be born

to the assumption that one could
just say, *It shall be*, and it would –
oh, nobody could have lived there
without a court,

mistresses, diaries, plots,
one would be bored too soon,
too soon, long for a hamlet
autrichien, built round a lake

where one could play milkmaids
until word came the people
marched against all this frippery.
Yet it's better

than the ugly huge wooden coffer
they would put Napoleon in
under a vulgar dome. The silkworm
is mortal but its lissom thread

insists, *I was*. If you left nothing
your first visit there are castles now,
not built in air but on eight
nights' bliss. They were. They shall be.

The coaches leave at midnight.
Twelve years ago, alone, you ran
like Cinderella. Now,
my empty glass shines like her shoe.

The Seine

Rain rips in one burst through the sky.
It blows the people off the terraces,
they crowd the zinc. When I arrived

in Paris, Paris
was out of town. Only maintenance crews
in shops and bars stayed on,

I half believed they all spoke English in the wings.
The stores are full of satchels, notebooks, pencils,
parenthood as a competition.

I remember how much got broken, stolen
or lost, and miss my children. Tears
pressure my eyes,

not that they'd quench the city's dust
or shift
this solitary drinker from his stool.

What moves me is the time.
Seventy years late
I want to miss the Montmartre dusk,

tired of the gynaecology
spread out for tourists. I métro
through Stalingrad (history!) for the other bank

where red clouds
are the city's reflected light
gathered, streetlamps, illuminated monuments,

pleasure-craft rocking
the river in its bed,
the invisible stars.

It's somehow comforting
to be tucked in like this, out in the open,
light being what it is, an evanescence.

I miss you
roars in me like the ocean in a shell.
Spotlights on Notre Dame

are nothing to the dark there,
the pools of candles, the one
I lit for us.

Light is an evanescence,
we are easily lost. A father
leans on a parapet

to watch the sway of water
pressing towards the sea.
The day you left

we saw frogmen
diving at a determined point.
I held your hand. I knew it wasn't you.

La Défense

The century will end
and we'll have made it
through to the next, if only
we can forget the future
we were promised in children's books and more

dismayingly,
the nothing it could come to.
We must go underground
to reach the smaller, airier Manhattan,
paradise for my afternoon's

modernistic way with your camera, glass
reflecting glass reflecting glass. Wind
blew across Paris, up
those stepped plazas, steppes
with the water and trees we cannot part with,

water bent artfully
down a falls of prismatic colour,
smooth water echoing
a column's blue
and its spiral of orange suns and rocks,

trees the size of orange-trees at Versailles
and saplings bordering
the square and makeshift playground
of Arab children. Wind
wanted to scrub the place clean

as it was in the planners' visionary eyes
and almost was. My old
headmaster's rule that every snapshot
demands a human frame for scale was true.
There were so few, I had to go for cars.

Some of the windows
have gold sealed into them,
conspicuous assumption
that nothing changes: money keeps
its nineteenth-century perspective here,

Haussmann's perspective on the Arc de Triomphe
diminished, distant but distinct. Think
of Victor Hugo
lying in state beneath it
before his pauper's funeral,

of story-telling, how it might change
what it's about.
Man's the measure
of nothing in a future made to measure; a Miró
sculpture without a context lit

flickers of interest
in windows when the clouds changed place.
Glass and water, water and glass,
repetitive
reflections of familiar names.

I have lost my footing in time.
We went, we saw
the nothing it could come to,
nowhere that could be anywhere.
The slot your shape left in my empty bed.

Le Cimetière de Montparnasse

At the end of the world there will be cats
crouched like police-cars in the rubble. They play
tag in this town of tiny oratories, this huddled
and atomised society. Whole families are buried
as one, often lying in the teeth of their lives

like Baudelaire, whose name, below his stepfather's,
above his mother's, is gripped by the jaws that ground him,
though so many solitary sorrows won't add up
to anything. In a square plot, a square slab
says TRISTAN TZARA 1896 + 1963

for whom no pxxm
sous rature
with la littérature
aeui
o   dada

the second word maybe of the one-year-old boy
put next to him. All one. I meant to bring a rose
for Sartre, who couldn't synthesise the flesh
and freedom any more than the woman who lies with him
in the narrowest bed. *Bonjour Simone* a note starts

under a pot of roses. The grave is littered
like Lycidas' with verses, flowers, letters,
no different from the *A notre grand-mère and A mon
arrière-grand-mère* plaques you can buy at the corner,
vulgar and trite and true. I saw cars looking

for relatives. One of the women's letters
was signed off with a row of crosses hung from circles,
fragility men made to signify the female.
It, or another, spoke of perpetual struggle,
though the idea that we could live for causes

puts the effect before the cause. We'll only know
afterwards if our lives meant anything or not,
or not know. For an hour or more I walked among the
   dead,
an hour or more I trod the hushing gravel
wondering why we live.

I was lonely, but nothing like the dead
are lonely, I was scared by all that bricolage of faiths,
the Cross, the Star of David, the blank disbelief.
The same mongrel cats kept crossing my path
over and over. Watch them. They are watching.

Outside the Luxembourg Gardens

Somewhere near Albuquerque
they dropped a nine-megaton bomb by accident
when I was ten months old. I wasn't there,
but if they'd had command by reflex
as they do now, I'd probably be nowhere,

certainly not here, sipping Pernods
in the bar of La Closerie des Lilas, waiting
for a table. No need to wait the night you came.
Everything's slowing up: I reached the Deux Magots
only a shade behind our shadows, but when I left

police had closed the Luxembourg Gardens. Whistles
harried the stragglers. Paris, Sarah, is closing
to us and opening to herself. The clientèle
tonight is mostly French, and the Métro was full
of Qantas labels. The only victim

the bomb had was a cow at the point of impact,
which we might well have called Ground Zero. I brought
    you here
because in nineteen-twenty-five a Russian emigrée
sat on the terrace every morning, ordered tea,
paper and ink (O times gone by! – though the girl next to
    me

reads today's papers in wooden spines, the way
we've read about) and wrote interminable letters.
I'm pretty certain what she called herself then,
not whom she wrote to, though the week you joined me
I spent mornings reading the printed evidence.

Anyway, call her Elsa Triolet. One morning
there was a ruckus in the bar I'm sitting in,
some item of surrealist doctrine, and somebody
pointed out to her Louis Aragon, whom she'd take,
later, in something like an armchair, willed

to have and hold him. Her eyes were *Les yeux d'Elsa*,
symbols of France resisting occupation. La Place du
Colonel Fabien, which we went to early on,
has the ex-directory communist headquarters.
The entrance is unmarked. Stalinism in concrete,

the foyer tilts, disorients you, makes you think
how easily people can disappear.
                                    The pianist starts
to stride, swinging into a fast blues. That *Elsa valse
et valsera* I know, but me, I think of Chuck Berry
riding through Albuquerque on his trip to the Promised
    Land.